-2

HAPPY HOME

Everyday Magic
for the Family Kitchen

Charlotte Hedeman Guéniau

Foreword by Paul Lowe

FOREWORD

I can still remember the first time I stepped into Charlotte's Rice world.
It was years ago at a trade show in Copenhagen. I found myself surrounded
by colors, lots of colors. And patterns. Pink plates with polkadots, bowls with flowers,
fun textiles and everything that will put a big smile on your face. I remember
wondering, who was the brain behind this crazy fun world? Then I met Charlotte
a few years later in New York and I totally understood why Rice is the way it is.
Rice is about being playful and real (Just like her).

Charlotte is the essence of colorful, a pure joy of life and I'm so happy
that she stepped into the food world with this book. I love her mantra
PLAY TOGETHER - STAY TOGETHER. It's really all about love, and food is love,
no doubt about it. It doesn't matter if you are making a simple Tuesday night
dinner or having a party: It's all about pleasure, love and creating. I love inviting
people over to my house. I often give them a chopping board, a knife and a glass
of wine. I do think chopping goes better with a glass of wine! And just because
I invite you to dinner does not mean I have to do all the work! Right?

I'm so happy to see Charlotte's ideas for this book, just up my alley.
I'm someone who thinks food and crafts go hand in hand (as I try to show
in my magazine), and am so excited to see that in this book. I grew up in a family
where cooking was one of the highlights of the day. My grandmother did most of it
and she let me help. So from an early age I could make homemade tomato sauce,
bake bread and whip up the occasional chocolate cake. So my mantra is LET YOUR
KIDS HELP (They might grow up having their own magazine).

So, send out the invites, make a playlist, buy some food and let's have a party.
And make my lemon and feta dip, you can find it on page 115. It's a winner!
Happy Party!

Paul Lowe
Founder and Editor in Chief of *Sweet Paul Magazine*

CONTENTS

PARTY TOGETHER

FUNKY TEA PARTY

DO IT YOURSELF

GATHERING

PUT THE EXTRA IN ORDINARY

CONDIMENTS: DIPS, CHUTNEYS, AND JAMS

HAPPY HOME
EVERYDAY MAGIC FOR THE FAMILY KITCHEN

Cooking - sharing - loving... It's pretty basic - and quite essential, yet sometimes seeing your friends for dinner becomes such a project... Most of us are running on a tight schedule - we manage to fill out our everyday lives with a bunch of activities on top of work - add all the daily routines like laundry, house cleaning, grocery shopping and cooking..... Often we do not give priority to meet up with friends and family and just do stuff together...

This book is meant as an inspiration to DO things together... and also to give you some recipes that make everyday lives easier...

Invite a few friends - have a great cooking session together. When the day is over you all go home with lots of nice food for the freezer or to give away as a nice present. Some of the ideas also come with a simple DIY that can be made by people of all ages. Creating things with kids is a fantastic way of spending time together. I find that some of the best talks arise on occasions like this, when everybody is focused on making something.

At the moment my house is blessed with loads of teenagers - I love to have them breezing in and out of our home - and I want to savour every moment as I am very well aware of how fast time flies by. Pizza night for example is a cozy and different night to share with that age group or any age group really...

One of my mantras is PLAY TOGETHER - STAY TOGETHER! That warm feeling inside when you spend time with the people you like hanging out with. Imagine that and then add something productive into the mix....things that you can enjoy now or later...

It's like the gift that keeps on giving...
Join in and let's create some Everyday Magic moments together.

"There is no love sincerer than the love of food."
George Bernard Shaw

PARTY TOGETHER

It's really about the fun...

Be it pizza night or build your own spring rolls...
it's a fun informal way to eat together.

All you have to do is chop, knead and roll everything in advance
and when the guests arrive everyone is in charge of their own
creations and can play according to their own taste buds.

I LOVE hosting pizza nights - they are just my kind of relaxed
and fun evenings. In summer time, I always throw the pizzas
on the bbq.

The fresh rolls are best if eaten within 24 hours, but the spring
rolls for frying are freezer-friendly. We looooove to keep a small
stock of spring rolls - they are a great idea for a cook-together.
It's more fun to do all the chopping when you are chatting along
with your friends during preparations.

"One cannot think well, love well, sleep well,
if one has not dined well."
Virginia Woolf

FRESH RICE PAPER ROLLS, COLOR ME HAPPY STYLE

Serves 4
Preparation time: 40 minutes

1 mango
4 radishes
1 large beet
1 red bell pepper
1 yellow bell pepper
1 avocado
2 carrots
2 small heads of cos lettuce
1 package rice paper wrappers
Mixed fresh herbs - mint and cilantro are always good ideas

Wash and peel the mango, radishes, beet, peppers, avocado, and carrots. Cut them into very small sticks. Wash the lettuce.

In a large bowl filled with hot water, place one wrapper. Let it soften for 10 seconds, then put it on a plate.

In the center of the sheet of rice paper, arrange a lettuce leaf and top it with 1 tablespoon of the mango and of each chopped vegetable and with a few leaves of the fresh herbs. Then wrap following the package directions.

Tip

You can add some cooked jumbo shrimp or chicken breasts (steamed and cut into thin slices) to this vegetarian version. Yours rolls will only be better!

CLASSIC SPRING ROLLS

Serves 6
Preparation time: 40 minutes
Cooking time: 20 minutes

For the spring rolls

1 small onion
1 clove garlic
2 carrots
3 stalks celery
6 stalks asparagus
1 red bell pepper
¼ red cabbage
7 ounces (200 g) string beans
1 teaspoon olive oil
2 tablespoons oyster sauce
1 teaspoon vegetable stock powder
1 package of Spring roll wrappers
Salt and pepper to taste
Oil for frying

For the sweet chili dip

¾ cup (200 ml) sweet chili sauce
Juice of ½ lime
(about 1 tablespoon)
Cilantro and scallion, finely chopped

Let's Roll! For the classic spring roll, I like to combine many different things. You can even use fried rice if you have leftovers. Or you can use the ground meat from the Easy Peasy Spicy Chicken Balls (page 74): Just place a spoonful on each wrapper. You can stir-fry a mix of different vegetables and make a vegetarian version, as we've done here.

Make the spring rolls: Peel and chop the onion and garlic. Wash and peel the carrots, celery, asparagus, pepper, cabbage, and beans, then cut them into small sticks.

In a wok or a large saucepan, heat the olive oil and sauté the onion and garlic. Add the carrots and stir-fry for 1 to 2 minutes, then add the rest of the vegetables. Toss everything well together. Add the oyster sauce, vegetable stock, salt and pepper. Stir-fry well. Remove from the heat and leave to cool a little.

Now you are ready to wrap up some delicious spring rolls. Place a spoonful of the filling on each wrapper and wrap following the package directions. In a frying pan, heat a generous amount of oil. Fry the wraps until crispy and golden.

Make the sweet chili dip: Stir the chili sauce, lime juice, cilantro, and scallion together and serve with the classic spring rolls.

Bon appétit

CLASSIC RED PIZZA SAUCE

Makes 10 pizzas
Preparation time: 15 minutes
Cooking time: 30 minutes

2 tablespoons olive oil
1 onion, finely chopped
3 cloves garlic, finely chopped
1 handful fresh basil leaves, chopped
1 teaspoon dried oregano
2 cans (14 ounces / 400 g each) tomatoes
1 small can tomato paste
Salt and freshly ground black pepper

This sauce is also a great base for a lot of other dishes, so make a generous amount and store it in the freezer.

In a large saucepan, heat the olive oil. Add the onion and garlic and stir. When the onion becomes translucent, add the basil, oregano, tomatoes, and tomato paste. Mash the tomatoes with the back of a spoon and let the sauce simmer on low heat for about 20 minutes. Add salt and pepper to taste.

If you want a smooth sauce, now is the time to puree it in a blender. After pureeing, pour the sauce back into the pan, bring it to the boil, turn down the heat, and let it simmer for 5 minutes to concentrate the flavors. If you prefer a chunkier sauce, just skip the blending and let it simmer.

When the consistency is the way you want it, and just perfect for spreading on your pizza, the sauce is done!

Tip!

For more flavor, add a pinch of cinnamon or 1 tablespoon of brown sugar.

PIZZA WITH CARAMELIZED ONIONS, BACON, MOZZARELLA, AND SOFT GORGONZOLA

Makes 1 small pizza
Preparation time: 15 minutes
Cooking time: 40 minutes

3 onions
2 tablespoons olive oil
Classic Red Pizza Sauce
(page 17)
1 store-bought tortilla
6 slices good-quality bacon
3½ ounces (100 g) soft
Gorgonzola cheese
1 mozzarella cheese ball
(about 5 ounces / 150 g), sliced
Fresh spinach leaves

Preheat the oven to 435°F (225°C).

Peel and slice the onions. In a frying pan, sauté them very slowly in the olive oil, on low heat, for about 30 minutes. The slow frying brings out the sweetness of the onion, so there is no need to add sugar.

Spread the red pizza sauce on the tortilla and scatter over it the caramelized onions, bacon, Gorgonzola, and mozzarella. Bake in the oven until the cheese has melted and is golden (about 10 minutes). Sprinkle with fresh spinach leaves and enjoy.

HEALTHY AND DELICIOUS GLUTEN FREE CAULIFLOWER PIZZA DOUGH

Makes 1 large pizza
Preparation time: 15 minutes
Cooking time: 25 minutes

For the dough
2½ ounces (70 g) pitted black olives
1 cauliflower
3½ ounces (100 g) mushrooms
2 eggs
Salt and freshly ground pepper to taste

For the topping
Miss Mitzi's White Pizza Sauce
10 slices zucchini
10 slices red onion
10 slices mushrooms
3½ ounces (100 g) grated Emmental cheese (optional)
1 clove garlic
Olive oil
Salt and pepper

This is a really soft, very healthy, and super tasty pizza dough.

Preheat the oven to 435°F (225°C).

Prepare the dough: In a bowl, combine the olives, cauliflower, mushrooms, and eggs and process them with a handheld blender (you can also pulse them in the bowl of a food processor). Place the dough on a sheet of parchment paper and flatten it using your fingers. Bake for about 12 minutes. Leave to cool a bit.

Prepare the topping: Spread Miss Mitzi's white pizza sauce all over the crust. Top with the zucchini, onion, mushrooms, and Emmental, if using, and season with salt and pepper. Bake again for about 10 minutes.

MISS MITZI'S WHITE PIZZA SAUCE

Makes 1 large pizza
Preparation time: 5 minutes

8¾ ounces (250 g) ricotta cheese
3½ tablespoons (5 cl) cottage cheese
1 tablespoon olive oil
2 cloves garlic, grated
Salt and freshly ground black pepper

This is really good when you make pizza bianca.

In a bowl, whisk the ricotta and cottage cheese together until well blended. With a handheld blender or in a mini food processor, pulse the ricotta mixture with the olive oil and garlic. Add salt and pepper to taste.

NAAN BREAD PIZZAS

Makes 4 small pizzas
Preparation time: 10 minutes
Cooking : 10 minutes

4 naan breads
Classic Red Pizza Sauce
(page 17)
8 slices prosciutto
1 mozzarella cheese ball
(about 5 ounces / 150 g), sliced
Fresh basil leaves

The naan bread you can buy at the supermarket is a great base for a lunch-pack pizza. This is a classic kid-friendly version with tomato sauce, ham, and cheese. Your kids will love you for it.

Preheat the oven to 435°F (225°C).

Simply spread the red pizza sauce on the naan breads.
Top with the prosciutto and mozzarella.

Bake in the oven for about 10 minutes until the cheese has melted and is golden. Sprinkle with fresh basil.

Have fun

MANGO-PASSION FRUIT SMILE

Makes 4 drinks
Preparation time: 15 minutes

1 mango
4 passion fruits
2 limes
3 sprigs fresh mint
Sparkling water

Peel the mango, then dice it into small cubes and divide them among four glasses. Cut the passion fruits into halves; put one half into each glass, and save the others for decoration. Add half a juiced lime to each glass, fill with the sparkling water, and garnish with the mint leaves.

>>>———— *Tip* ————▶

If you like your drinks a bit on the sweet side,
you can add 1 teaspoon of cane sugar.

RHUBARB RUMBLE

Makes 1 drink
Preparation time: 5 minutes

2½ tbsp (40 ml) rhubarb syrup
1 cup (250 ml) sparkling water
2 slices of lemon

This drink truly tastes like summer and pink skies...

In a tall glass pour the syrup and sparkling water over ice cubes.
Add lemon slices - stir and enjoy.

FUNKY TEA PARTY

Every girl dreams of having a fabulous afternoon tea party,
just like the one in *Alice in Wonderland*.

I would like to inspire you to go all in: Think big and organize
a modern and funky afternoon tea party with every girly girl
you know, no matter how young or old. I love to hang out with
women of all ages; there is something about it that makes a lot
of sense. From three years old to ninety-five is my favorite
age group. The recipes here are a bit slimmed down from
the traditional tea party menu, to keep you from falling asleep,
all heavy and full, or getting into a sugar-induced frenzy.

"Don't grow up, it's a trap."

Peter Pan

SPONGY LEMON CAKE WITH POPPY SEEDS

Serves 6
Preparation time: 25 minutes
Cooking time: 55 minutes

⅓ cup (75 g) unsalted butter, plus more for the pan
1¼ cups (250 g) sugar
½ ounce (15 g) poppy seeds
Freshly grated zest of 1½ lemons (about 4 teaspoons)
⅝ cup (150 ml) milk
1¾ cups (225 g) wheat flour
2 teaspoons baking soda
½ teaspoon salt
3 egg whites
Edible flowers

For the lemon syrup
½ cup (100 ml) water
Freshly squeezed juice (about 3 tablespoons) and grated zest (about 3 teaspoons) of 1 lemon
¼ cup (50 g) sugar

For the lemon frosting
Freshly squeezed juice of 1 lemon (about 3 tablespoons)
2 cups (250 g) confectioners' sugar

This lemon cake is the perfect mix of soft, sweet and sour, and spongy — a retro cake loved by every generation.

Preheat the oven to 340°F (170°C).

Prepare the cake: In a bowl, beat together the butter, sugar, poppy seeds, and lemon zest until well combined. Gradually pour in the milk and continue beating until incorporated. In another bowl, combine the flour, baking soda, and salt, then add one-third of the flour mixture at a time to the butter mixture. Beat until the batter is light and fluffy. In a clean bowl, beat the egg whites until stiff peaks form. Gently fold them into the batter until well mixed, but without stirring too much. Pour the batter into a well-greased 10½-inches (26 cm) round cake pan and smooth the surface. Bake for 45 minutes. The cake is done when it springs back when lightly pressed.

Prepare the lemon syrup: While the cake is baking, combine in a saucepan the water, lemon juice and zest, and sugar. Bring to a boil at low heat. Then turn up the heat and let boil until the mixture has a syrupy consistency.

Pour the syrup over the cake as soon as the cake comes out of the oven. Let it cool for a while before turning it out onto a wire rack to cool completely.

Prepare the frosting: Combine the lemon juice and the confectioners' sugar to a pourable consistency.

Place the cake on a platter sprinkled with a bit of confectioners' sugar to avoid sticking. When the cake is completely cold, spread the frosting all over and sprinkle poppy seeds and the edible flowers on top.

ROCKY ROAD

Makes 30 pieces
Preparation time: 10 minutes
Cooking time: 5 minutes
Refrigeration time: 4 hours

1 pound (500 g) dark chocolate
9 ounces (250 g) Snickers
or other caramel bars
14 ounces (400 g) salted peanuts
8 ounces (225 g) mini
marshmallows
Freeze-dried raspberries,
crumbled

The way to Rocky Road is simple — it's straight, not long and winding.
Make these part of your celebratory traditions. You can vary them by using different nuts, or dried fruit in place of the mini marshmallows — just play, and you will always rock everybody's taste buds.

Melt the chocolate in a bain-marie. Cut the caramel bars into bite-size pieces.

In a large bowl, combine caramel bars, peanuts and marshmallows. Pour the melted chocolate over them and quickly stir together, making sure everything is covered in chocolate. Pour onto a baking tray lined with grease-resistant paper, sprinkle with the freeze-dried raspberries, and put in the fridge for a few hours.

Once the mixture has set, cut into squares, or desired size. Store in the fridge.

DATE BALLS

Makes about 12 balls
Preparation time: 10 minutes
Cooking time: 5 minutes
Refrigeration time: 4 hours

3½ ounces (100 g) pitted dates
1¾ ounces (50 g) chopped
almonds
¼ teaspoon vanilla sugar
or vanilla extract
1 teaspoon orange peel
(optional)
Grated coconut

Put the dates and almonds in a food processor or a blender and process on high speed until the mixture is smooth.
Add the vanilla sugar and orange peel, if using, and mix well.

Shape into balls, or desired size. Roll the balls in the grated coconut until well covered. Refrigerate for a few hours.

>>> —— *Tip* —— ►

For a funky look, add a few drops of food coloring to the grated coconut and stir well. These healthy date balls also look amazing if rolled in crumbled freeze-dried raspberries.

MERINGUES

Makes 24 to 30 roses
Preparation time: 30 minutes
Cooking time: 1 hour 30

2 egg whites
1 teaspoon lemon juice
1 cup (140 g) confectioners'
sugar
Food coloring (optional)

Preheat the oven to 210°F (100°C).

In a bowl with the mixer at slow speed, beat the egg whites until they start to foam, then add the lemon juice. Whip at high speed until soft peaks form. Add sugar one spoon at a time and keep beating until the sugar has completely dissolved and the meringue is firm. Now add any food coloring you like, and as much as you like, if using.

Line a baking sheet with grease-resistant paper. Spoon the mixture into a piping bag fitted with a star tip and make the roses by holding the tip at a ninety-degree angle to the sheet and piping a spiral beginning at the center and working outward. Bake for 1 hour 30 minutes. Let cool completely before serving.

Store the meringues in an airtight tin.

COLORFUL VANILLA MILKSHAKES

Serves 4
Preparation time: 10 minutes
Cooking time: 5 minutes

2 cups (500 ml) good-quality
vanilla ice cream
1¼ cups (300 ml) milk
Seeds from 1 vanilla pod
A few drops food coloring
Water or lemon juice
Sprinkles

Put the ice cream and milk in a blender. Scrape the seeds from the vanilla pod and add them to the mixture. Blend until mixture is smooth and frothy. Add the food coloring and stir until the color is even and to your liking.

Dip the rims of four glasses first in the water or lemon juice and then in the sprinkles of your choice. Pour the milkshake into the glasses and serve right away.

>>>———— *Tip!* ————►

You can further garnish the shake with whipped cream
and chocolate sprinkles on top.

BEET QUICHE

Serves 6
Preparation time: 20 minutes
Cooking time: 1 hour 20

For the filling
1¾ pounds (750 g) beets
3½ ounces (100 g) bacon
4½ ounces (125 g) feta cheese
5 eggs
1 cup (250 ml) sour cream
2 teaspoons thyme leaves
Salt and freshly ground pepper

For the crust
2⅓ cups (300 g) graham flour
3¼ cups (300 g) flour
3 teaspoons salt
⅔ cup (150 ml) olive oil
1¼ cups (300 ml) water
Butter for the pie dish

Preheat the oven to 390°F (200°C).

Prepare the crust: In a large bowl, combine the graham flour, flour, and salt and mix in the oil using your fingers. Add most of the water and lightly knead the dough. Roll out the dough and place in a greased 12½-inches (32 cm) pie dish. Trim the edges with a sharp knife. Poke the crust with a fork and pre-bake it for 15 minutes.

Turn down oven to 360°F (180°C).

Prepare the filling: Peel and grate the beets. Fry the bacon until crisp, and crumble the feta cheese.

In a bowl, beat the eggs and sour cream well together and add the grated beets, bacon, and feta. Season with the thyme, and with salt and pepper to taste. Pour onto the pre-baked crust and bake again for 1 hour. Serve immediately.

Cool

OPEN-FACED SANDWICHES, BRUSCHETTA STYLE

There's really not much of a recipe for these, as they're something you can make according to your mood and favorite taste. The basic ingredients needed are slices of a nice bread (we used a classic baguette), cottage or cream cheese, and any topping you like.

We made the following varieties:

1. Cottage cheese with avocado, mixed roasted seeds, and lemon zest.

2. Cream cheese with Sun-Dried-Tomato Pesto (page 118) and a drizzle of parsley oil.

3. Cream cheese with thinly sliced radishes and fresh chives.

4. Cream cheese with shrimp, lemon juice, salt, and freshly ground pepper.

5. Cream cheese with salmon and pepper.

6. Cream cheese with hardboiled eggs and dill.

You can't really do anything wrong with these. Just follow what your heart and stomach desire.

Happy happy

Do it yourself

CHOCOLATE KISSES

These are such a sweet and easy thing for kids to make

You will need

Chocolate — any variety you like • Ice cube or chocolate molds

1 Cover the bottoms of the molds with the sprinkles.

2 Melt the chocolate over a hot-water bath or in a microwave oven.
Pour it into the molds.

3 Let the chocolates cool and harden completely before removing them
from the molds.

Do it yourself

GLITTERY STRAW DECORATIONS

You will need

Piece of paper • Pencil to trace the shapes • Glitter foam sheets
• Paper punch or hand punch • Scissors • Straws

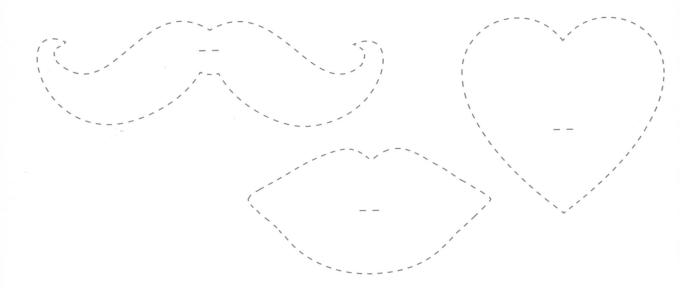

1. You can either scan the templates directly from this page or trace them onto a piece of paper and cut them out.

2. Use a template to draw the desired shape on the back of a glitter foam sheet. Cut it out. Punch a hole in the middle and insert the straw.

3. You can use any kind of craft paper — it does not have to be glitter foam sheets.

Do it yourself

PASTEL SUGAR LUMPS

You will need

Sugar • Food coloring • Water • Small ice cube or chocolate molds

1. Pour the sugar into a bowl.
   Ask an adult to preheat the oven to 180°F (80°C) degrees.

2. In a glass, mix the food coloring with water.
   Add 1 teaspoon at a time to the sugar and blend thoroughly.
   The texture should be like wet sand.

3. When the texture is right, put the sugar into the molds. Be sure to press
   it down firmly.

4. Ask an adult to bake in the oven for 10 minutes. Keep an eye on it,
   so the sugar doesn't melt. Remove from the oven and let dry for a day.
   Gently remove from the molds — you have the sweetest sugar lumps!
   Put them in a nice jar and give them as a little gift to someone you like.

Do it yourself

STONE ALPHABET

You will need
Smooth stones • Markers or acrylic paint • Glitter glue • Lacquer

1 Make sure the stones are clean by washing them in warm water with a little soap. Let them dry before starting to paint.

2 Paint the letters with the markers or acrylic paint and decorate with the glitter glue.

3 For a long-lasting result, you can give the stones a coat of the lacquer when they are completely dry.

Do it yourself

DRINKS COVERS

You will need
Pegboards · Perler beads · Parchment paper · An iron

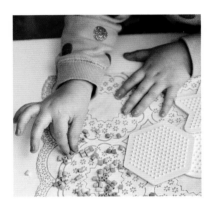 

1 Choose a pegboard. We used a round pegboard, but you can pick any shape as long as it is big enough to cover the glass.

2 Place the beads in the design you want, but remember to leave out one or two beads at the center of the pegboard. This is the hole you put the straw through.

3 Get some parchment paper and carefully place it over the beads on the pegboard. Ask an adult to preheat a dry iron to a medium temperature and slowly move it in a circular motion until the beads have melted together. Remove the parchment paper and then carefully remove the pegboard. Let cool completely before pushing a straw through the hole.

Do it yourself

ICE CREAM GARLAND

You will need

Cardboard in all the colors you like
• Pencil to trace the shapes • Paper punch
or hand punch • Glue • Glitter glue
• Pom-poms • String • Scissors

1 Trace the patterns for the ice cream
and the cone onto the cardboard and cut out
as many as you want for your garland. Punch
out holes for the string.

2 Glue the "cones" and the "ice creams"
together and let dry. Let your fantasy run
wild: Decorate the "ice creams" with glitter
glue for some extra sparkle and glue a
pom-pom at the top.

3 Pull the string gently through the punch
holes and make a little loop at each end
for easy hanging.

Do it yourself

CUPS DECORATION

You will need

1 cup per person • Glue • Glitter glue • Pom-poms • Stickers• Washi tape • Markers

This is really all about letting you inner artist out. The cups can be decorated in any way you like. We made faces, but anything goes. Just remember that these are strictly for decoration — they will not survive a washing.

Do it yourself

BEAUTIFUL ICE CUBES WITH EDIBLE FLOWERS

You will need

Ice cube trays in any shape or size you like • Small edible flowers

1 Just pour the water into the ice cube tray and very gently place the flowers on the surface. Put in the freezer until completely frozen. This way, the flowers will look like they're floating on the surface of the ice cube.

2 If you want the flowers to be in the middle of the ice cube, fill the tray halfway with water. Put in the flowers and wait until the water is frozen. Then add more water to cover the flowers and freeze again.

Do it yourself

YELLOW REFRESHING ICE CUBES

You will need

Orange juice • Ice cube trays in any shape or size you like

1 Just pour the orange juice into the tray and put it in the freezer until the cubes are frozen.

2 You can make these with any kind of juice you like, or you can add some fresh mint leaves or chunks of fruit as an extra nice touch.

Have fun ➤

Do it yourself

SAY MY NAME FRUIT STICKS

These are a great way to customize your party

You will need

Yellow fruit such as melons, mangos, apples, or pineapples
• Cutters in all letter shapes • Wooden skewers

1 Prepare the fruit by cutting it into fairly thin slices.

2 Cut the slices into the desired shapes using the cutters.

3 Gently push the fruit letters onto the wooden skewers — you can write your name or any message you want!

GATHERING

A few generations back, it was normal for people to meet up and cook together, to help one another, when a cow had been slaughtered, to cut, cure, and salt the meat, in preparation for winter.

I really like this idea and feel that everyone goes home enriched after a day like this. You can gather friends for a "jam session". Everyone brings ten pounds of different kinds of fruit and some jars — and you make delicious chutneys and jams all day.

You drink, chat, chop, have fun, and share the result. You can also hold a "big meal-prep party" where the idea is to fill the freezer with meat loaf or soup.

"People who love to eat are always the best people."
Julia Child

HOW TO THROW A BIG MEAL-PREP PARTY . . .
FOR GIFTS AND FOR THE FREEZER

This is a short guide you can use for organizing one of these fun gatherings. It has a few useful tips and tricks to get you started, whether the theme of the day is baking, soup making, or other great freezer meals.

1/ GATHER A GROUP OF FRIENDS

Gather four or five friends who share your love of cooking, having fun, and just being together!

2/ DESIGNATE A "BOSS OF THE DAY"

It is a good idea to choose a designated leader for the day in order for things to run smoothly. You can also decide that each person will make his or her own recipe. The main idea is to have fun, hang out, and be productive all at the same time.

3/ WHERE TO MEET

Pick the person in your group who is most relaxed about having a house full of people and a messy kitchen. All the others can bring their own knives and chopping boards.

4/ WHAT TO MAKE

Decide on a theme. Ask the people involved to come up with one or two recipes per participant. It is a good idea to start with just one recipe per person until you have tried this a few times. First-time success is important. The recipes can then be multiplied accordingly, so that each person will go home with four to five freezer meals in total.

5/ KEEP IT SIMPLE...

Personally, I find it easiest when every-one shops for his or her own recipe — in triple or quadruple quantities, according to how many you are. But if you want to do it a different way, everyone can bring grocery receipts and you can work it out when you're together.

6/ THE PACKAGING...
NOT TO BE FORGOTTEN

I like the idea of using these meals as gifts. I would be delighted if someone came to my house and brought me a homemade frozen meal. Make sure you have enough containers for the production of the day. Think fun labels and nice jars and freezer boxes. Each person should bring printouts of recipes for everyone else to take home.

7/ LET'S GET THIS PARTY STARTED

Now is when the fun really begins. What needs to be prepped first? Work it out and find a way that suits you. Perhaps you will find it easiest to make just one or two recipes at a time in order not to get all the ingredients mixed up. If the weather allows it, I love to sit outside, prepping the vegetables or fruit.

8/ ENJOY THE MOMENT

Chop, chat, laugh, and remember to enjoy the process and appreciate that you get to hang out and catch up with your friends at the same time!

FABULOUS MEATLOAF

Serves 6
Preparation time: 20 minutes
Cooking time: 1 hour 10

⅓ cup (150 ml) coconut milk
⅓ cup (150 ml) chopped parsley
2 stalks celery, chopped
½ pound (250 g) ground pork
½ pound (250 g) ground beef, (or 1 pound (500 g) ground beef and omit ground pork)
1 egg
⅓ cup (150 ml) oats
1 clove garlic, grated
2 carrots
¼ celery root
½ pound (250 g) spinach, fresh or frozen
½ teaspoon grated nutmeg
2 teaspoon salt
1 teaspoon freshly ground pepper
8 slices bacon
Butter for the pan

Preheat the oven to 425°F (220°C).

In a bowl, combine the coconut milk, parsley and celery stalks. In another bowl, combine the ground meat with the egg, oats, and garlic. Add the coconut milk mixture to the meat.

Peel and grate the carrots and celery root. Thaw the spinach if you use the frozen kind, or roughly chop the leaves if you use fresh. Add to the meat mixture. Season with the nutmeg, salt, and pepper. Grease the mold you like. Shape into a loaf, and bake for 50 to 60 minutes.

Dice the bacon, fry it until crisp, and sprinkle it on top of the meatloaf about 10 minutes before it is done.

Serve with a nice salad and some freshly baked crusty bread.

Tip

This tastes delicious with sweet chili sauce on the side.

FUNKY MEATBALLS WITH SWEET KISS SAUCE

Makes about 60 meatballs
Preparation time: 30 minutes
Cooking time: 10 minutes

For the meatballs

1 pound (500 g) ground beef

2 tablespoons olive oil

2 teaspoons lightly crushed sesame seeds

13 tablespoons (200 ml) bread crumbs, or 7 tablespoons (100 ml) oats

2 teaspoons grated fresh ginger

2 cloves garlic, grated

4 green onions, chopped

1 carrot, grated

1 red chile, finely chopped (optional)

1 teaspoon salt

1 teaspoon pepper

For the Sweet Kiss Sauce

7 tablespoons (100 ml) hoisin sauce

5 tablespoons neutral vinegar, such as rice vinegar

2 cloves garlic, chopped or grated

2 tablespoons sesame oil or olive oil

1 tablespoon sesame seeds

1 tablespoon grated fresh ginger

2 green onions, chopped

3½ tablespoons (½ dl) fresh cilantro, chopped

Meatballs — every country has its own version of these, and they seem never to go out of fashion. These versions are fabulous and very easy to love and make. These are great served as appetizers, in a buffet, or as a main dish. The sauce comes with a warning: Watch out! The sweetness makes it very kid-friendly — and highly addictive.

Preheat the oven to 425°F (220°C).

Make the meatballs: In a bowl, combine the beef, olive oil, sesame seeds, bread crumbs, ginger, garlic, green onions, carrot, chile, if using, salt, and pepper. Mix well together. Shape into bite-size balls and place them on a baking sheet or in a greased pan. Bake for about 10 minutes.

In the meantime, prepare the sauce: In a bowl, combine the hoisin sauce, vinegar, garlic, oil, sesame seeds, ginger, green onions, and cilantro and whisk together. Put aside some of the chopped green onions and cilantro for garnishing the meatballs.

Place the meatballs on a nice dish, pour some of the Sweet Kiss Sauce over them, and sprinkle the reserved cilantro and green onions on top. I like to add chili flakes as well, for that extra bite, but this is of course optional. My experience is that you can teach your children very early on that spicy food is great stuff. I always think of how Thai children, for instance, love chiles and spicy food. It's all a matter of training.

Tip!

Place a toothpick in each meatball. This makes them fun to look at and easy to grasp without kids' hands getting all sticky.

EASY PEASY SPICY CHICKEN BALLS

Makes about 45 chicken balls
Preparation time: 20 minutes
Cooking time: 20 minutes

2 pounds (1 kg) ground chicken
½ cup (120 ml) soy sauce
½ cup (120 ml) sweet chili sauce
1 cup (200 ml) oats
10½ ounces (300 g)
grated carrot
9¾ ounces (275 g) grated
celery root
9¾ ounces (275 g) sweet potato,
peeled and grated
2 cloves garlic, grated
2 eggs
1 tablespoon grated fresh ginger
1 teaspoon chili flakes
3 teaspoons (50 ml) chopped
parsley

These chicken balls are always a success. You can customize the recipe by adding any vegetable you have in your fridge — the more the merrier. What I love about them is that they are so easy to make: Just pop them in the oven — no oil or grease needed.
Warning: Always make a lot more than you think you need. Everyone finds them irresistible, and before you know it they are all gone.

Preheat the oven to 425°F (220°C).
In a bowl, combine the chicken, soy sauce, sweet chili sauce, oats, carrots, celery root, sweet potato, garlic, eggs, ginger, chili flakes, and parsley. Mix well together and shape into meatballs.
Place on a baking sheet lined with parchment paper and bake for 18 to 20 minutes.

Serve with peanut dressing (page 121).

>>> ——— *Tip* ———▶

These meatballs are very easy for parents and children to make together.
Kids love mixing the meat with their bare hands
and afterward placing the balls in straight lines on the baking tray.

Serve with Sweet Potato Hummus (page 112) or, for an Asian touch, with teriyaki, sweet chili sauce, chopped coriander, and finely sliced green onion.

BASIC BOLOGNAISE

Serves 6
Preparation time: 10 minutes
Cooking time: 30 minutes

2 onions
4 carrots
4 stalks celery
2 tablespoons olive oil
2 cloves garlic, grated
1 pound (500 g) ground beef
1 tablespoon tomato puree
6 sprigs fresh thyme
1 handful fresh oregano
2 cans of diced tomatoes
(about 14 ounces / 400 g each)
Salt and pepper

*The basic meat sauce, or bolognaise, is an all-time winner.
Our version is a bit sneaky, as it is full of vegetables — something
that a lot of kids normally refuse to eat, just out of principle —
but hidden in a bolognaise, anything goes. And the kids can easily
be part of the making. Let them do the easier tasks, such as peeling
the carrots or chopping the celery stalks. Very often, children are
much more inclined to taste, and like, food that they have helped
make.*

*I love the idea of making a huge amount and dividing it into
smaller portions for the freezer. And when you take out a batch
of your basic recipe, you can use it in so many different ways:
As it is or in a lasagna, or you can add kidney beans and some
Mexican spices and — voilà! — you have a nice chili con carne.
Use it for our Quesadilla Snack (page 78) or to make lovely
samosas. The options are endless. Just do whatever you feel
like doing.*

Dice the onions, carrots, and celery. In a large saucepan, heat
the oil and briefly sauté the garlic. Add the ground beef and stir
until the meat is browned all over. Pour in the diced vegetables
and the tomato puree, thyme, and oregano and let simmer
for 5 minutes. Add the diced tomatoes and let simmer for another
20 minutes. Add salt and pepper to taste.

If the sauce is too thin, you can either use a little cornstarch
to thicken it or — if you have the time — let it simmer until
the texture is right.

Tip!

If fresh herbs are not available, the dried versions will be just as fine,
but use only one-third the amount.

Add some bay leaves for a deeper, more rounded flavor.
Just remember to remove them before serving.

QUESADILLAS WITH BASIC BOLO AND MANGO-AVOCADO SALSA

Makes 4 quesadillas
Preparation time: 20 minutes
Cooking time: 25 minutes

For the quesadillas
8 round tortillas
(store-bought is fine)
3½ ounces (100 g) grated
Cheddar cheese
Basic Bolognaise (page 77)

For the salsa
1 ripe mango
1 avocado
½ red chile or bell pepper
½ green onion, chopped
Salt and pepper

Use a portion of the Basic Bolognaise (page 77) and some store-bought tortillas for a very delicious and easy appetizer, or just as a quick snack.

Heat a tortilla in a pan. Flip it after a short time and add some of the grated Cheddar and a thin layer of the bolognaise. Place another tortilla on top, and, after a little while over the heat, flip the whole thing and give it 30 to 45 seconds on the other side.

Prepare the salsa: Finely dice the mango, avocado, chile, and green onion and toss together. Add salt and pepper to taste.

Cut the quesadillas into slices and serve with the lovely mango and avocado salsa.

ROASTED BUTTERNUT SQUASH AND MANGO SOUP WITH PARSLEY AND BASIL OIL

Serves 6
Preparation time: 20 minutes
Cooking time: 45 minutes

1½ pounds (700 g) butternut
squash, peeled, seeded,
and cut into small chunks
1 onion, coarsely chopped
1 clove garlic, peeled
and chopped
3 large tomatoes
(about 9 ounces / 250 g)
or good-quality canned
tomatoes, coarsely diced
7 ounces (200 g) potatoes,
peeled and cut into chunks
½ fresh red chile, seeded
and chopped
Juice of 1 lime
(about 2 tablespoons)
2 heaping teaspoons
mango chutney
5 cups (1.2 l) vegetable stock
Parsley and Basil Oil (page 118)
Olive oil
Salt and pepper

Preheat the oven to 390°F (200°C).

Place the diced squash on a baking tray and drizzle with a little olive oil. Bake for about 20 minutes or until tender.

Meanwhile in a large saucepan, splash some olive oil and cook the onion, garlic, tomatoes, and potatoes until the onion is soft and the tomatoes cooked to a pulp.

Add to the saucepan the baked squash and the chile, lime juice, chutney, and vegetable stock and let simmer until the potatoes are tender.

While the soup is simmering you can make the parsley and basil oil (page 118).

Blend the soup until velvety and smooth. Add salt and pepper to taste. Pour into bowls and drizzle with beautiful, green parsley and basil oil.

>>>———— *Tip* ————▶

Roast some pumpkin and sesame seeds and sprinkle on top of the Parsley and Basil Oil to dress up the soup.

IRISH WINTER WARMER SOUP

Serves 4
Preparation time: 15 minutes
Cooking time: 45 minutes

1 onion
1 clove garlic
2 tablespoons olive oil
3 large parsnips
4 carrots
1 heaping teaspoon turmeric
4½ cups (1 litre) vegetable stock
Salt and pepper

Finely chop the onion and garlic. Add to a saucepan heated with 1 tablespoon of the olive oil. Stir until the onions and garlic are softened and translucent.

Dice the parsnips and carrots and add them to the pan, stirring well to make sure they are coated with oil. Add the turmeric and season with salt to taste. Stir well again, making sure everything is covered in turmeric. Cover the pan with the lid and let simmer on low heat for 10 minutes, stirring occasionally to prevent burning. Pour in vegetable stock and simmer for another 20 to 30 minutes. In a blender or food processor, process the soup until smooth. Return to pan and reheat.

Sprinkle with a bit of olive oil and black pepper, and serve with some brown bread or crusty white bread.

>>>———— *Tip!* ————►

Perfect on a cold day! Turmeric is anti-inflammatory and a great immune-system booster.

CAULIFLOWER AND CELERY ROOT SOUP

Serves 6
Preparation time: 15 minutes
Cooking time: 25 minutes

1 cauliflower
¼ celery root
5 cups (1.25 litre) vegetable stock
1¼ cups (300 ml) cream or milk
Sunflower seeds
Croutons
Salt and pepper

Chop cauliflower and celery into small pieces and put in a saucepan together with the vegetable stock. Bring to a boil and let simmer for 20 minutes or until the vegetables are tender. Add cream and blend the soup until it is smooth and velvety.
Add salt and pepper to taste.

Roast the sunflower seeds on a hot, dry frying pan for a few minutes until they are lightly golden. Sprinkle the soup with the seeds and croutons.

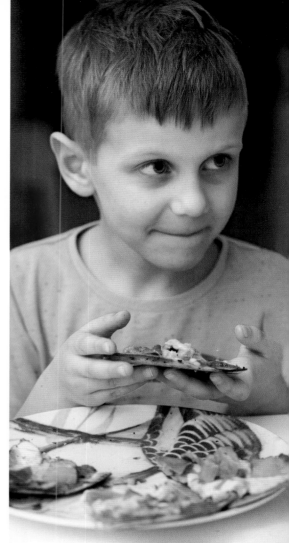

PUT THE EXTRA IN ORDINARY

A fun way to invite guests is to choose a color theme.

It doesn't take much extra effort and it is loads of fun to prepare. A yellow evening, a red night, a white dinner...you could even ask you guests to dress in the chosen color.

Many years ago my family and I lived in the country side and during summer the fields around our house were bright yellow. This inspired me to invite for a yellow dinner - it was simple, but such a joy, and an evening none of us will ever forget. Eating yellow food, having yellow drinks and being completely surrounded by fields of yellow colza.

"I want it all — and I would like it delivered."
Bette Midler

DEVILED EGGS APPETIZER

Serves 4
Preparation time: 15 minutes
Cooking time: 10 minutes

6 hardboiled eggs
¼ cup (60 ml) mayonnaise
1 teaspoon Dijon mustard
½ teaspoon chipotle chile
5 drops Tabasco®
¼ teaspoon salt

Carefully cut the hardboiled eggs in half lengthwise and gently remove the yolks. In a bowl, mash the yolks with the mayonnaise, Dijon, chipotle, and Tabasco until you get a smooth texture. Add salt to taste. Pipe or spoon the filling into the hollowed-out egg whites.

Tip

You can dye the egg whites with food coloring for a fun and colorful look.
Put food coloring into a bowl and add some water.
Now simply place the halved egg whites in the bowl until tinted to the tone you like — this will take only a few minutes.
If the color is too pale, just add more coloring. Drain on paper towels.

CHICKEN CURRY IN A HURRY

Serves 4
Preparation time: 15 minutes
Cooking time: 25 minutes

1 pound (500 g) boneless
chicken breast
1 onion
1 clove garlic
1 tablespoon olive oil
3 heaping teaspoons
curry powder
1¼ cups (300 ml) coconut milk
7 tablespoons (100 ml)
vegetable stock
1 yellow bell pepper
Fresh cilantro (optional)
Salt and pepper

Cut the chicken breast into bite-size pieces. Chop the onion and garlic and in a saucepan sauté in the olive oil until translucent. Sprinkle with the curry powder and mix well.

Add the chicken to the pan and continue stirring for a few minutes. Pour in the coconut milk and vegetable stock. Add salt and pepper to taste — and extra curry, if desired. Leave to simmer for 10 to 15 minutes.

Wash and seed the bell pepper and cut into long, thin strips. Throw them into the pan a few minutes before serving so that they remain crispy.

Sprinkle the dish with fresh cilantro, if using, and serve.

YELLOW-ME-HAPPY RICE

Serves 4
Preparation time: 10 minutes
Cooking time: 25 minutes

1 onion (second onion optional)
1 clove garlic
1 ounce (30 g) butter
2 tablespoons ground turmeric
8¾ ounces (250 g) rice
4½ cups (1 l) vegetable stock
3½ ounces (100 g) canned corn
Salt and pepper

Chop 1 onion and the garlic. In a saucepan, heat the butter and fry the onion and garlic with the turmeric for a few minutes. Add the rice and sauté until nicely colored and a bit translucent. Add the vegetable stock and season with salt and pepper to taste.

Bring to a boil and then reduce to medium heat. Cover the pan with a lid. Simmer for about 20 minutes until the rice is tender.

Remove from heat, add the corn and the second onion, finely chopped, if using. Fluff the rice with a fork and serve.

So good

GO FOR THE FUN VEGGIES

Serves 4
Preparation time: 15 minutes
Cooking time: 20 minutes

1 onion
3 yellow carrots
2 yellow or soft green squash
1 tablespoon olive oil
1 ounce (30 g) grated
Parmesan cheese
Salt and pepper

Chop the onion. Cut the carrots and squash into thin slices.

In a saucepan, stir-fry the onion in the olive oil. Add the carrots and squash and stir-fry for 5 minutes. Season with salt and pepper to taste. Add the Parmesan and toss together.

Serve with the yellow rice (page 94) and the chicken curry (page 93).

Bon appétit

GRETHE'S AMAZING LEMON MOUSSE

Serves 6
Preparation time: 20 minutes
Refrigeration time: 2 hours

5 gelatin sheets
4 large organic
or pasteurized eggs
6¼ ounces (175 g) sugar
7 tablespoons (100 ml)
freshly squeezed lemon juice
1½ teaspoons finely grated
lemon zest
1¼ cups (300 ml) whipping
cream

This dessert — even when I read the recipe my mouth waters. It's a classic, old-fashioned dessert, but it really hits the spot every time. Grethe's version is the best and easiest I have ever come across.

In a bowl, soak the gelatin sheets in cold water, making sure they are covered. In another bowl, whisk the eggs and sugar until they become thick and creamy. Add the lemon juice and lemon zest. Beat together until well combined.

Lift the gelatin sheets along with the water that clings to them (no squeezing!). Put them into a heat-resistant bowl and let them melt over a hot-water bath.

Pour the melted sheets into the egg-and-sugar mixture in a high, thin stream while beating vigorously. Whip the cream until soft peaks form (save a little for garnishing) and gently fold it into the mixture. Pour the mousse into six portion-size glasses or a large bowl and place in the fridge for at least 2 hours.

Garnish with the reserved whipped cream before serving.

Mon chéri

PRETTY PERFECT PINK STARTER

Serves 4
Preparation time: 20 minutes

¼ fennel bulb
½ pomegranate
2 slices watermelon
7 ounces (200 g) cold-water
shrimp, shelled
A few sprigs cilantro or parsley
1 tablespoon good-quality
olive oil
Salt and pepper

This is a very tasty and funky combination — and a feast for the eye at the same time.

Cut the fennel bulb into very thin slices — use a mandoline, if you have one. Put them into a bowl and squeeze a little pomegranate juice over them (reserve the seeds). Toss together and let rest while you prepare the remainder of the recipe.

Cut the watermelon slices in half and garnish them with the fennel, shrimp, reserved pomegranate seeds, and cilantro.

Drizzle with the olive oil and add salt and pepper to taste. Serve the feta dip (page 115) on the side.

Tip!

You can also add chunks of nice, soft feta on top of the watermelon slices.

PINK TZATZIKI

Preparation time: 10 minutes

10½ ounces (300 g) peeled
and grated raw beetroot
1 pound (500 g) Greek yoghurt
1 clove of garlic
Salt and pepper

*This tzatziki is a fun and tasty version of the greek recipe
with grated cucumber, finely cut mint leaves and dill.
Can easily be made the day before – it only tastes better!*

Peel and grate the beetroot. Mix in with yoghurt, grated garlic,
salt and pepper. Place in the refrigerator.

For a fresh and colorful touch, sprinkle with edible flowers.

Tip

This tzatziki tastes delicious with a salmon fillet or Pink Sesame Potatoes
(page 105), it is also great as a Sandwich or Bruschetta Spread (page 42).

SIMPLY SALMON
WITH PINK SESAME POTATOES

Serves 4
Preparation time: 20 minutes
Cooking time: 30 minutes

1 pound (500 g) small potatoes
4 tablespoons sesame seeds
Approx. 1¾ ounces (800 g)
salmon fillet
Red food coloring
Olive oil
Pink Tzatziki (page 102)
Salt and pepper

Preheat the oven to 425°F (220°C).

Wash the potatoes thoroughly, wipe them and put them
in an oven dish. Drizzle with olive oil and salt. Bake in the oven
for 15 minutes.

Meanwhile, pour the sesame seeds into a small bag and add
a few drops of red food coloring. Shake the bag until the seeds
are evenly colored and put aside for later.

Put the salmon in an oven dish. Season it with salt, pepper,
and a slush of olive oil. Bake for approx. 15 minutes
with the potatoes until nicely golden and tender.

Serve the salmon immediately with the pink tzatziki and the potatoes
generously sprinkled with the pink sesame seeds.

>>>——— *Tip !* ———►

Serve with a pink/red themed salad.

PINK PAVLOVAS

Makes 8 to 10 pavlovas
Preparation time: 30 minutes
Cooking time: 1 hour 30

Meringue (page 36)
Red food coloring
13 tablespoons (200 ml)
whipping cream
7 oz (200 g) pink
or red fresh berries

Meringue is everybody's darling. Size really doesn't matter.
You can make these pavlovas big or portion-size, as you please.

Preheat the oven to 210°F (100°C).

Prepare the meringue and add a few drops of the food coloring
to make it pink. Using a spoon, set a mound of meringue on a sheet
of parchment paper. Flatten it gently with the back of the spoon
until it reaches the desired thickness (¾–1¼ inches / 2–3 cm).

Bake for 1 hour 30 minutes.

While the meringues cool completely, whip the cream and wash
and trim the berries. Ladle a generous spoonful of whipped
cream on each meringue and garnish with the berries.
Serve right away.

CONDIMENTS: DIPS, CHUTNEYS, AND JAMS

Dips, dressings, salsas, pestos... spreads...
You name it. It's often the little things that make the big
difference when you serve a meal, or make a sandwich.

I find that I can always take a meal to a higher level if I have a few
dips or spreads in stock. Whipping up a pesto or a hummus
is equally quick. Make a double portion so you always have
a small stock in your fridge. Even the simplest steak or fish filet
will get that little extra if dipped into a hummus or a nice pesto...

I also love to serve these as snacks with different raw vegetables
or small biscuits – it's a great snack starter.

"No one is born a great cook, one learns by doing."
Julia Child

ALL-AROUND-SNACK SEED CRACKERS

Makes 40 crackers
Preparation time: 10 minutes
Cooking time: 15 to 18 minutes

7 tablespoons (100 ml) oats
7 tablespoons (100 ml)
sesame seeds
7 tablespoons (100 ml) flax seeds
7 tablespoons (100 ml)
sunflower seeds
7 tablespoons (100 ml)
pumpkin seeds
1½ cups (350 ml) flour
1 teaspoon baking soda
2 teaspoons salt
⅜ to ⅝ cup (100 to 150 ml) oil
⅞ cup (200 ml) water

*These healthy seed-filled crackers are easy to make.
And if you store them in an airtight container, you can keep
them for weeks — if you can keep away from them.*

Preheat the oven to 390°F (200°C).

In a bowl, combine the oats, sesame seeds, flax seeds, sunflower
seeds, pumpkin seeds, flour, baking soda, and salt. Add the oil
and water and mix well. The mixture should be very sticky.
Roll out half the mixture between two sheets of parchment paper,
until about ⅛ inch (3 mm) thick. Gently remove the top sheet
and slice the crackers into the desired size and shape with
a sharp knife. Do the same with the other half of the mixture.

Bake for 15 to 18 minutes until golden brown.

Let the crackers cool completely before storing in an airtight
container.

Tip

A nice jar of these makes a great little present.
Just dip in...

SWEET POTATO HUMMUS

Preparation time: 10 minutes
Cooking time: 45 minutes

2 large sweet potatoes

1 can chickpeas (8½ ounces /
240 g drained)

1 large clove garlic

Juice of 1 lemon
(about 3 tablespoons)

4 heaping tablespoons tahini

1 teaspoon cinnamon

2 tablespoons olive oil

1 tablespoon cumin

2 teaspoon brown sugar
(optional)

1 teaspoon cayenne pepper
or 1 heaping teaspoon
dried chili flakes

Sesame seeds

Preheat the oven to 425°F (220°C) and bake the sweet potatoes for about 45 minutes until tender. Leave to cool.

In a food processor, combine the chickpeas, garlic, lemon juice, tahini, cinnamon, olive oil, cumin, and brown sugar, if using. Once the potatoes have cooled, peel the skin off and add the potatoes to the processor bowl. Process well until smooth.

Pour into a bowl, garnish with a light sprinkle of cayenne pepper and sesame seeds for a great finishing look, and serve!

Serve with a tortilla or any Middle Eastern flatbread
and lots of freshly cut vegetable sticks.

If you leave the hummus in the fridge for several days,
you might need to re-spice it slightly. Over time it can lose a bit of taste.

SWEET PAUL'S FETA DIP

Preparation time: 15 minutes

14 ounces (400 g) feta cheese

2 tablespoons grated lemon zest, plus more for garnish

2 to 4 tablespoons fresh lemon juice

2 cloves garlic, minced

6 tablespoons extra-virgin olive oil, plus more for serving

1 pinch red pepper flakes

In a blender, combine the feta, lemon zest, 1 tablespoon lemon juice, garlic, and olive oil and pulse until combined but still slightly chunky. The dip is dense, so you may need to stir it with a fork once or twice. Taste and, if it's too salty, add more lemon juice.

Spoon into a serving bowl, drizzle with a little olive oil, and garnish with a pinch of the pepper flakes and some lemon zest. Serve with crudités, chips, toasts, pita crisps, or seed crackers (page 110).

Tip

Add a little finely grated fresh ginger for extra bite.

GO GO GO GREEN PESTO WITH CASHEW NUTS

Preparation time: 15 minutes

1¼ cups (300 ml) flat parsley, packed

⅞ cup (200 ml) cilantro, packed

7 tablespoons (100 ml) olive oil

7 tablespoons (100 ml) cashew nuts or peanuts

Salt and freshly ground pepper

Dried chili flakes

Take two cups of any fresh herbs you have — and here I really do mean any. I love to mix and modify and just use whatever I have when I make a green pesto. I love to use a mix of parsley, cilantro, chives, dill, and mint, and sometimes even arugula, if I have some. The recipe below calls for parsley and cilantro, but I really mean it when I say just play — you cannot make a mistake.

Wash the parsley and cilantro. In a blender, combine them with the olive oil, and nuts and pulse until smooth.
Put into a jar and store in the fridge.

Tip

I like to add a bit of grated Emmental cheese, which I just mix in by hand after the pesto is pulsed, and also some coarsely chopped capers, if I have some.

ROASTED GARLIC PARMESAN HUMMUS

Preparation time: 15 minutes
Cooking time: 40 minutes

1 bulb garlic
6 tablespoons (90 ml) olive oil
1 can good-quality chickpeas
(about 14 ounces / 400 g),
reserving some of the liquid
6 tablespoons (90 ml) tahini
1¾ ounces (50 g) freshly grated
Parmesan cheese
¼ teaspoon cumin
Juice of 1 lemon
(about 3 tablespoons)
Chopped flat parsley
Dried chili flakes (optional)
Sea salt
Freshly ground pepper

This hummus is like the kiss of an angel: It's as smooth as velvet, and the roasted garlic gives it a very sweet taste. Sometimes I cook the chickpeas myself, but I find it rather time-consuming and not very conducive to spontaneity.

Preheat the oven to 425°F (220°C).

Cut the top off the bulb of garlic, sprinkle with the olive oil, and wrap in aluminum foil. Bake for about 40 minutes. Let cool a bit and squeeze out the cloves.

In a food processor, combine the chickpeas, tahini, Parmesan, cumin, and lemon juice and pulse until texture is creamy. If the hummus feels too dry, just add a bit of the water reserved from the chickpeas. Add salt and pepper to taste.

Pour the hummus into a bowl and sprinkle with the parsley and, if you want a bit of extra spice, the dried chili flakes.

MY "SAVE THE DAY" SUN-DRIED TOMATO PESTO

Preparation time: 15 minutes

10½ ounces (300 g) sun-dried tomatoes in olive oil

2 cloves garlic, coarsely chopped

13 tablespoons (200 ml) fresh basil

1¾ ounces (50 g) grated Parmesan cheese

1 small handful black olives

4 tablespoons (60 ml) pine nuts or any other nut you have

2 tablespoons capers

Extra-virgin olive oil

Salt and freshly ground black pepper

Pesto is often my savior. If the fridge is getting empty, but you have some pasta on hand, just add a nice pesto and you're back in business. I like to have a few pestos around for a rainy day. This great condiment can easily replace a traditional sauce, and it's lovely as a spread on a sandwich or in a wrap, or you can combine a bit of hummus with it and yummmmyyyy it's even more delicious.

In a food processor, process the sun-dried tomatoes and their oil with the garlic, basil, and Parmesan until the tomatoes are finely chopped but still have some texture. Add more oil if needed to reach the desired consistency.

Add the olives, pine nuts, and capers and pulse a few more times. I like these to remain a bit chunky in the pesto. Add salt and pepper to taste.

Tip!

Store the pesto in the refrigerator, or freezer, in an airtight container or jar.

PARSLEY AND BASIL OIL

Preparation time: 15 minutes

2 large handfuls fresh flat-leaf parsley

2 large handfuls basil leaves

⅝ cup (150 ml) good-quality olive oil

Juice of ½ lime (about 1 tablespoon)

Salt and freshly ground pepper

Wash the parsley and basil. In a food procesor, pulse them with the olive oil and lime juice into a smooth oil.

Add salt and pepper to taste.

VINA'S MAGIC GARLIC DRESSING

Preparation time: 15 minutes
Cooking time: 10 minutes

2 teaspoons cooking oil
4 cloves garlic, finely chopped
1 teaspoon chili flakes
7 tablespoons (100 ml) soy sauce
Juice of ½ lemon
(about 1½ tablespoons)

In a small saucepan, heat the oil on low heat. Sauté the garlic until it is dark brown. Then add the chili flakes and stir. Turn off the heat and add the soy sauce and lemon juice. Stir everything together well. It's ready to serve.

PEANUT DRESSING FOR COLORFUL FRESH SPRING ROLLS

Preparation time: 15 minutes

1 onion, finely chopped
1 clove garlic, finely chopped
2 tablespoons sesame oil
6 heaping tablespoons crunchy peanut butter
1 medium red chile, seeded and finely chopped
⅝ cup (150 ml) water
3 tablespoons fish sauce
Juice of 1 lime
(about 2 tablespoons)

In a saucepan, sauté the onion and garlic in the sesame oil. Add the peanut butter, red chile, water, fish sauce, and lime juice and let boil for a few minutes. Adjust the taste with extra chile, if you wish.

Let cool before serving.

⟫⟫⟫———— *Tip* ————▶

This dressing also works very well with chicken or fish.

SPICY CARROT GINGER CHUTNEY

Preparation time: 30 minutes
Cooking time: 30 minutes

1¼ pounds (550 g) peeled
and grated carrots
1 cup (250 ml) minced onion
2 tablespoons freshly
grated ginger
1 cup (250 ml) apple
cider vinegar
1 cup (250 ml) water
6 ounces (170 g) brown sugar
1 teaspoon dried thyme
½ teaspoon cayenne pepper
Juice and zest of 1 large lemon
1 teaspoon salt
¼ teaspoon freshly ground
pepper

In a large saucepan, combine the carrots, onion, ginger, cider vinegar, water, brown sugar, thyme, cayenne pepper, lemon juice and zest, salt, and pepper. Bring to a boil over high heat. Stir continuously, to avoid burning, for 5 minutes.

Reduce heat and let simmer for about 20 minutes, until the mixture thickens. Leave to cool and then put into sterilized jars. If you can wait, let the chutney mature for a few days. It is even better when the flavors have had time to fully develop.

PLUM AND PINEAPPLE CHUTNEY

Preparation time: 30 minutes
Cooking time: 15 minutes

2½ pounds (1.2 kg) plums
1 onion
14 ounces (400 g) pineapple
1 chile, seeded
5 cloves
1 stick cinnamon
13 tablespoons (200 ml) vinegar
14 ounces (400 g) brown sugar

I love chutneys — they are such charmers in your mouth, and on your plate. Sweet and spicy at the same time, a chutney can really lift even the simplest dinner to a whole new level. This one goes really well with fish, pork, and white meats.

Pit the plums and cut them into quarters. Chop the onion into thin wedges. Cut the pineapple into small pieces and finely chop the chile.

In a saucepan, sauté the cloves and cinnamon stick for a few minutes. Add the vinegar and brown sugar and bring to a boil for about 5 minutes. Reduce heat and let simmer for another 5 minutes. And voilà! Leave to cool and then put into sterilized jars.

Tip!

If you find the chutney too runny, you can add a bit of pectin
and boil it for an extra minute or two before pouring the chutney into jars.

CHIA SEEDS FREEZER STRAWBERRY JAM

Preparation time: 25 minutes
Refrigeration time: 24 hours

1¾ pounds (800 g) strawberries
4 tablespoons honey
6 tablespoons chia seeds
Juice of 1 lemon
(about 3 tablespoons)

Almost too easy. Because no cooking is involved in the preparation, you will preserve the taste of fresh, sun-ripened strawberries, but the jam will not stay fresh forever, so keep in the fridge only as much as you will eat in a few days, and freeze the rest.

Gently rinse the strawberries before hulling them. In a food processor or blender, puree the strawberries, honey, chia seeds, and lemon juice.

Pour into containers of suitable size and place in the fridge. The jam will be ready to eat in a few hours, when the chia seeds have worked their magic.

Tip

Wait twenty-four hours before putting the containers in the freezer. Then you can just pull out a fresh batch whenever the urge hits you. But be fast if you want to freeze some — my son thinks this is the best jam I have ever made.

CARROT AND ORANGE JAM

Preparation time: 25 minutes
Cooking time: 45 minutes

5 organic oranges
2 pounds (1 kg) carrots
Zest of 1 orange
(1½ tablespoons)
2 cups (500 ml) water
1 vanilla pod, halved
and scraped
10½ ounces (300 g) brown sugar
3 teaspoons pectin

Wash the oranges and remove the peels. Chop the peels finely and put them in a saucepan. Peel off the white rind on the oranges and discard. Chop the oranges roughly.

Add the oranges, carrots, orange zest, water, and vanilla pod to the saucepan and let simmer for about 20 minutes.

Add the brown sugar and let boil for another 10 to 20 minutes until the jam becomes translucent and the ingredients are tender. Add the pectin and let boil for 2 more minutes. Remove from heat, let cool a little, and then put into sterilized jars.

RICE AROUND THE WORLD

AUSTRALIA
Corner Store
147 South Terrace (cnr Price St)
Fremantle WA 6160
0061 8 9336 3005
www.cornerstore.net.au

Corner Store
201-205 Stirling Highway
(cnr Loch St) Claremont WA 6010
0061 9286 2280
www.cornerstore.net.au

AUSTRIA
Klammerth
J. K. Klammertth Josef Hahn's Erben
Herrengasse 7-9
8010 Graz
0043 316 8256180
www.klammerth.at

ediths
Lustenauerstr. 10
6850 Dornbirn
0043 5572 202569
www.ediths.at

Plastichouse
Goldschmiedgasse 4-6
1010 Wien
0043 1 5338211
www.plastichouse.at

BELGIUM
Zao
Rue du Bailli 96
1050 Bruxelles
0032 2 534 38 32

CHINA
Mothers Work
L-VDM-20, Level 1
SOLANA Shopping Mall No. 6
Chaoyang Park Road
Beijing 100125
0086 188 1086 2900
www.motherswork.cn

DENMARK
FineNordic.dk
Moeskjærvej 2
7620 Lemvig
www.finenordic.dk

RICETERIA by RICE
Mageløs 1
5000 Odense
0045 88 97 35 35

Invi2
Strandvejen 456
6854 Henne Strand
0045 75 25 50 60
www.invi2.dk

Continental
St. Sct. Peder Stræde 5
8800 Viborg
0045 86 61 43 24

Forvandlingskuglen
Skånegade 7
2300 København S
0045 36 30 66 66

Hesselholt
Hulsigvej 19
9990 Skagen
0045 98 44 64 42
www.galleri-hesselholt.dk

Lirum Larum Leg
Engholmvej 16
3100 Hornbæk
0045 70 26 98 90
www.lirumlarumleg.dk

Mandrup Poulsen Tapeter
Rantzausgade 1B
9000 Ålborg
0045 96 25 85 05

FRANCE
Le Petit Souk
13, rue de Paris
59000 Lille
0033 3 20 51 94 43
www.lepetitsouk.fr

Mon showroom
www.monshowroom.com

Smallable
www.smallable.com

Bonton
5, boulevard des Filles-du-Calvaire
75003 Paris
00 33 1 42 72 34 69
www.bonton.fr

Loulou Addict
25, rue Keller
75011 Paris
0033 1 49 29 00 61
www.loulouaddict.com

Le Panier d'Églantine
6, Grand-Rue
54000 Nancy
0033 3 83 20 61 47
www.lepanierdeglantine.com

Trait d'union
22, place Portalis
83270 Saint-Cyr-sur-Mer
0033 4 94 26 24 78
www.traitdunion-saintcyrsurmer.com

Zazou
4, rue du Colonel-Picot
29200 Brest
0033 2 98 46 21 90
www.zazou-boutique.fr

Le Grand Comptoir
4, rue Pagès
92150 Suresnes
0033 1 42 04 11 00
www.legrandcomptoir.com

Fleux'
39, rue Sainte-Croix-de-la-Bretonnerie
75004 Paris
0033 1 42 78 27 20

GERMANY
Kunterbunt & Zuckerstube
Lange Strasse 47
31515 Wunstorf
0049 5031 912260
www.kunterbunt-spielzeug.de

Das Tropenhaus
www.das-tropenhaus.de

Lorey
Schillerstr. 16
60313 Frankfurt am Main
0049 69 299950
www.lorey.de

Geliebtes Zuhause
www.geliebtes-zuhause.de

Grüner Krebs
Erbprinzenstr. 21
76133 Karlsruhe
0049 721 25 542
www.gruenerkrebs.de

Kontrast Frankfurt City
Kornmarkt 7
603141 Frankfurt am Main
0049 69 90 439 30
www.kontrastmoebel.de

RICETERIA by RICE
Schulstr. 2
70173 Stuttgart
0049 711 22980

Carl Abt GmbH & Co.KG
Münsterplatz 7
89073 Ulm
0049 731 163333
www.abtshop.de

Michaelsen Scandinavian Living
Hüxstrasse 62
23552 Lübeck
0049 451 88998020
www.michaelsen-living.de

Siller & Laar GmbH & Co.KG
Philippine-Welser-Str. 30
86150 Augsburg
0049 821 502810
www.siller-laar.de

Nostalgie im Kinderzimmer
www.nostalgieimkinderzimmer.de

Eat more cake
Westfleth 13
21614 Buxtehude
0049 4161 7809747
www.eatmorecake.de

HONG KONG
Mirth Home
The Mezzanine Floor, Yip Kan St.
Wong Chuk Hang
00852 25539811
www.mirthhome.com

IRELAND
Avoca
11-13 Suffolk Street
Dublin 2
00353 16774215
www.avoca.ie

Avoca
Rathcoole, Fitzmaurice
N7 Naas Road
Dublin
00353 12571800
www.avoca.ie

Avoca
The Mill at Avoca Village
Co. Wicklow
00353 40235105
www.avoca.ie

Avoca Kilmacanogue
Bray Co. Wicklow
00353 12867466
www.avoca.ie

Avoca Letterfrack Connemara
Co. Galway
00353 9541058
www.avoca.ie

Avoca Moll's Gap, Kenmare
Co. Kerry
00353 6434720
www.avoca.ie

The Garden Pavilion
Myrtle Hill Ballygarvan
Co. Cork
00353 214888134
www.thepavilion.ie

ISRAEL
Sofi
3 Nakhman st. Shuk
Pishpeshim
68138 Tel Aviv
00972 35162077

ITALY
Mettalia Cose di Casa
Via Roma 82
23 032 Bormio (so)
0039 0342 901625

Gallina Smilza
Via Santo Stefano 14d
40125 Bologna
0039 0515870640
www.gallinasmilza.it

Ristorante Don Claudio
Via Ugo Foscolo 61
30017 Jesolo (VE)
0039 0421375219

Athesia
Via Goethe 5
39100 Bolzano
0039 0471081135
www.athesia.it

JAPAN
Momo Shop
2-12-30 Higashikaigankita
Chigasaki-shi
Kanagawa 253-0053
0081 467 83 2424
www.momoshop.jp

MEXICO
El Palacio de Hierro
Coyoacán
Centro Coyoacán
Av. Coyoacán No. 2000
Col. Xoco C.P
03330 México D.F
0052 5422 1900
www.elpalaciodehierro.com

El Palacio de Hierro
Durango
Durango No. 230
Col. Roma Norte C.P
06700 México D.F
0052 5242 9000
www.elpalaciodehierro.com

El Palacio de Hierro
Santa Fe
Vasco de Quiroga No. 3800
Col. Vista Hermosa, C.P.
1257-9200
0052 5257 9200
www.elpalaciodehierro.com

NETHERLANDS

Heerlijck Thuis
Grote Kerk Straat 7
5911 CG Venlo
0031 77 3513008
www.heerlijckthuis.nl

Lant van Texsel
Vaalderstraat 23
1791 EB Den Burg
0031 222 322 031
www.winkeloptexel.nl

Nijhof
Minervaweg 3
3741 GR Baarn
0031 35 548 6192
www.nijhofbaarn.nl

Zinin
Burg. Reigerstraat 11
3581 KJ Utrecht 0031
030 251 8178
www.zininshop.nl

Dames van de Thee
www.damesvandethee.nl

Teitloos
www.teitloos.nl

NORWAY

Frøken Rosa
www.frokenrosa.no

Traktøren Bogstadveien A/S
Bogstadveien 25
0355 OSLO

Hakallegarden
6149 Åram
047 7001588
www.hakalleberte.no

Rafens
Sørensen 16
0159 Oslo
047 91745415
www.rafens.no

Ting Bergen
Bryggen 13
5003 Bergen
047 55215480
www.tingbutikken.no

Ting Oslo
Akersgata 18
0158 Oslo
047 22424242
www.tingbutikken.no

Randesund Lysstøperi & gavelof
Holteveien 138
4639 Kristiansand

SINGAPORE

The Childrens Showcase
200 Turf Club Road
#02-06/K45 Singapore
0065 6474 7440

The Childrens Showcase
Tanglin Mal
#03-08A Singapore
0065 6474 7440

SOUTH KOREA

Brandneo
1F 5-10, Apgujeong-ro 50-gil,
Gangnam-gu
135-897 Seoul
0082 23446 6535
www.styliti.com

SPAIN

Suit Beibi
Benet Mateu 52
08034 Barcelona
0034 93 205 72 60
www.suitbeibi.com

SWEDEN

Artiklar
Fleminggatan 65
112 32 Stockholm
0046 8 652 93 35
www.artiklarsthlm.se

Boink
www.boinkstore.com

Inreda
www.inreda.com

Milq
Gamla Brogatan 26
111 20 Stockholm
0046 8 411 32 50
www.milq.se

R.O.O.M Stockholm
Täby Centrum
106 37 Stockholm
0046 8 692 50 00

Slättarps Gård
Skegrie
231 93 Trelleborg
0046 733835995

Style4 Solutions AB
Verkstadsg. 3
59933 Ödeshög
0046 73 0279049

Syster Lycklig
Tegnergatan 12
113 58 Stockholm
0046 8 612 65 64
www.systerlycklig.se

Jollyroom
www.jollyroom.se

SWITZERLAND

Ademas
Garnmark 1
8400 Winterthur
0041 52 212 24 23
www.ademas.ch

Ars Longa
Bahnhofplatz 3
8001 Zürich
0041 44 211 22 02
www.arslonga.ch

The Home Shop
Rain 14
5000 Aarau
0041 62 823 49 46
www.thehomeshop.ch

Lieblings
Vordergasse 47
8200 Schaffhausen
0041 52 620 12 57
www.lieblings.ch

Werkeria
Bahnhofstr. 20
7000 Chur
0041 81 250 40 45
www.werkeria.ch

De la Suite dans les Idées
Rue de la Madeleine 14
1003 Lausanne
0041 21 312 34 59

Duo sur Canapé
Rue de Verdaine 10
1204 Genève
0041 22 311 22 41

Dédé et Charlotte
Rue de Lausanne 46
1700 Fribourg
0041 79 776 99 49

UNITED ARAB EMIRATES

Pantry Cafe
A1 Wasl Square
Al Safa
1 Dubai
00971 4 388 3868
www.pantrycafe.me

UK

Burford Garden Center
Shilton Road
Burford OX18 4PA
0044 1993 823117
www.burford.co.uk

Cherryade
180 Bridport Road Poundbury
Dorchester DT1 3BN
0044 1305266400
www.cherryadestore.co.uk

Fig 1
51 St Lukes Road
Bristol BS3 4RX
0044 117 3308167
www.fig1.co.uk

Fuego
5A Coombe Street
Lyme Regis
Dorset DT7 3PY
0044 1297 443933
www.fuegoshop.co.uk

Gazebo
74 High Street
Totnes TQ9 5SN
0044 1803 863679
www.whatalovelyshop.co.uk

Indian Summer
624c Fulham Road
Parsons Green
London SW6 5RS
0044 207 731 8234
www.indiansummershop.com

Oliver Bonas
129 Kensington High Street
London W8 6SU
0044 207 937 4686
www.oliverbonas.com

The Orchid House
15 Lake Road
Keswick CA12 5BS
0044 17687 72875
www.theorchidhouse.net

Sisters Guild
32 Catherine Hill
Frome, Somerset BA11 1BZ
0044 1373 455080
www.sistersguild.co.uk

The Whiting Post
The Clothes Horse
58 Harbour Street, Whitstable
Kent CT5 1AG
0044 1227 275900
www.thewhitingpost.com

LORDS
84-86 Holland Park Avenue
London W11 3RB
0044 207 243 4284
www.lordsathome.com

USA

Go Living
1152 Arroyo Avenue
San Carlos, CA 94070
001 650 716 6010
www.goliving-us.com

Huset
1316 1/2 Abbot Kinney Blvd
Venice, CA 90291
001 424 268 4213
www.huset-shop.com

Originals
261 Sound Beach Avenue
Old Greenwich, CT 06870
001 203 461 2290
www.originalslifestyle.com

Sockerbit NY
89 Christopher Street
New York, NY 10014
001 212 206 8170

Sockerbit LA
7922 West 3rd Street
Los Angeles, CA 90048
001 323 951 0402
www.sockerbit.com

Book Culture
450 Columbus Avenue
New York, NY 10024
001 212 595 1962
www.bookculture.com

CouCou
24 Union Park Street, South End
Boston, MA 02118
001 617 936 4082
www.coucou-boston.myshopify.com

Yolk
1626 Silverlake Blvd
Los Angeles, CA 90026
001 323 660 4315

Shop Sweet Lulu
702 Center Road
Frankfort, IL 60423
001 815 464 6264
www.shopsweetlulu.com

ACKNOWLEDGEMENTS

I spend fifteen years of my life in Paris – but for the last eighteen years I have been back in Denmark. When I was asked to write this book for La Martinière I was of course proud and pleased. It's been fun and interesting, to work in "the French way" again... connecting my past with my future. This is my 6th book and I hope you will enjoy it as much as I have enjoyed making it. It is a tribute to friends, food, good times and get-together.

I could not have managed without a fabulous and extremely helpful team. Especially thank you to Miss Mitzi Nielsen - for eagle eyes, words, and taking on the role of the organized excel person even if you don't love it. You did great. Loved working with photographer Stine from Skovdal & Skovdal again. Thank you to Lus and Mitzi for great DIY performance. We form a great team...

Photographs: Skovdal & Skovdal (Stine Christensen www.skovdal.dk)
Graphic design: Éléonore de Beaumont
ISBN: 978-1-4197-2517-3

Originally published in French in 2016 under the title *Happy Cooking : Cuisiner, Partager, Aimer*
by Éditions de La Martinière Jeunesse, a division of La Martinière Groupe, Paris

Printed and bound in Portugal by Printer Portuguesa, August 2016.